AF087632

Kids Living Green

Let's Save Energy!

by Jenna Lee Gleisner

Bullfrog Books

Ideas for Parents and Teachers

Bullfrog Books let children practice reading informational text at the earliest reading levels. Repetition, familiar words, and photo labels support early readers.

Before Reading
- Discuss the cover photo. What does it tell them?
- Look at the picture glossary together. Read and discuss the words.

Read the Book
- "Walk" through the book and look at the photos. Let the child ask questions. Point out the photo labels.
- Read the book to the child, or have him or her read independently.

After Reading
- Prompt the child to think more. Ask: There are so many ways to save energy every day. What can you do to help?

Bullfrog Books are published by Jump!
5357 Penn Avenue South
Minneapolis, MN 55419
www.jumplibrary.com

Copyright © 2019 Jump! International copyright reserved in all countries. No part of this book may be reproduced in any form without written permission from the publisher.

Library of Congress Cataloging-in-Publication Data

Names: Gleisner, Jenna Lee, author.
Title: Let's save energy! / by Jenna Lee Gleisner.
Description: Minneapolis : Jump!, Inc., [2019]
Series: Kids living green
Includes bibliographical references and index.
Audience: Ages 5–8. | Audience: Grades K to 3.
Identifiers: LCCN 2018035668 (print)
LCCN 2018037589 (ebook)
ISBN 9781641284585 (e-book)
ISBN 9781641284561 (hardcover : alk. paper)
ISBN 9781641284578 (pbk.)
Subjects: LCSH: Energy conservation—Juvenile literature. Classification: LCC TJ163.35 (ebook)
LCC TJ163.35 .G55 2019 (print) | DDC 333.791/6—dc23
LC record available at https://lccn.loc.gov/2018035668

Editor: Susanne Bushman
Designer: Molly Ballanger

Photo Credits: tetsuomorita/iStock, cover; KK Tan/Shutterstock, 1; Tony Stock/Shutterstock, 3; andras csontos/Shutterstock, 4; Avalon Studio/Getty, 5; Robert Dant/Alamy, 6–7; Lopolo/Shutterstock, 8–9; Sergey Novikov/Shutterstock, 10; Thomas M Perkins/Shutterstock, 11; Michael H/Getty, 12–13; Yarygin/Shutterstock, 14t; bestv/Shutterstock, 14b; uniquely india/Getty, 14–15; Fortish/iStock, 16, 23br; bruev/iStock, 17; Lisa-Blue/iStock, 18–19 (background); Image Source/iStock, 18–19 (foreground); pixdeluxe/iStock, 20–21; michaeljung/Shutterstock, 22; Elnur/Shutterstock, 23tl; zhangyang13576997233/Shutterstock, 23tr; Toa55/Shutterstock, 23br; princessdlaf/iStock, 24.

Printed in the United States of America at Corporate Graphics in North Mankato, Minnesota.

Table of Contents

Unplug	4
Let's Do It!	22
Picture Glossary	23
Index	24
To Learn More	24

Unplug

Let's save energy! Why?

It helps keep Earth clean.

How can we help?

Jack turns the light off when he leaves the room.

He does not leave it on.

Grant helps make dinner.
He closes the refrigerator.
He does not leave it open.

Cars can pollute.
Alex bikes to school.

Eve walks.

Zoey and her mom do not run the dryer.

They hang clothes.

The air and sunshine dry them.

Nice!

Mae helps put in new light bulbs.

They use less energy.

energy-saving light bulbs

We use solar lights.
The sun powers them!

solar light

They light our yard.

We turn off our screens.
We play outside instead.
It is fun!

You can save energy, too.
How will you do it?

Let's Do It!

Lessen Your Carbon Footprint

Your carbon footprint is the amount of greenhouse gases you give off. These gases heat and harm Earth. Carbon dioxide is a greenhouse gas. Humans give off carbon dioxide. Things we do or the way things are made give these gases off, too. Like what? Using energy. Using a car or flying in a plane.

Have an adult help you figure out what your family's carbon footprint is.

Go to:

http://meetthegreens.pbskids.org/features/carbon-calculator.html

Answer the questions honestly.

What did you learn about your carbon footprint? How do you think you could use less energy every day to lessen your carbon footprint on Earth?

Picture Glossary

dryer
A machine that dries clothing.

energy
Power from coal, electricity, or other sources that makes machines work and produces heat.

pollute
To make dirty or impure, especially with waste or other products produced by humans.

solar lights
Outdoor lights that use solar cells to gather sunlight and change it into electricity.

Index

bikes 10
dryer 13
Earth 5
energy 4, 14, 20
light 7, 17
light bulbs 14
pollute 10
refrigerator 8
screens 19
solar lights 16
sunshine 13, 16
walks 11

To Learn More

Finding more information is as easy as 1, 2, 3.
❶ Go to www.factsurfer.com
❷ Enter "let'ssaveenergy!" into the search box.
❸ Click the "Surf" button to see a list of websites.